S Corporation Tax Secrets for Beginners 2024

Strategies for Small Business Owners to Slash Their Tax Bills and Unleash the Hidden Potential of S Corporations for Maximum Tax Savings

GREGORY SMITH

Dear Reader,

Thank you for embarking on this journey to delve into the intricate world of S corporation taxation. Your decision to invest your time and energy into mastering these essential concepts is truly commendable. By arming yourself with the knowledge and insights contained within these pages, you are taking proactive steps towards financial empowerment and success.

As you navigate through the contents of this book, know that your dedication to learning and growing as a small business owner is the driving force behind every word written.

Your commitment to understanding the nuances of S corporation tax laws is a testament to your ambition and foresight.

It is with deep appreciation that I extend my gratitude to you for choosing to explore the strategies, tips, and techniques presented here.

May the wisdom gained from these pages serve as a valuable asset in your journey towards maximizing tax savings and achieving your financial goals.

With warm regards,
Gregory Smith.

Copyright © 2024 by GREGORY SMITH

All rights reserved. No part of this publication may be reproduced, distributed, or transmitted in any form or by any means, including photocopying, recording, or other electronic or mechanical methods, without the prior written permission of the publisher, except in the case of brief quotations embodied in critical reviews and certain other noncommercial uses permitted by copyright law.

CONTENTS

INTRODUCTION — 14

   THE IMPORTANCE OF TAX PLANNING FOR SMALL BUSINESSES — 16

CHAPTER 1 — 20

UNDERSTANDING S CORPORATION — 20

CHAPTER 2 — 28

THE BASICS OF S CORPORATION TAXATION — 28

CHAPTER 3 — 38

TAX BENEFITS OF S CORPORATION — 38

CHAPTER 4 — 46

STRATEGIES FOR OPTIMAL SALARIES AND DISTRIBUTION — 46

CHAPTER 5 — 54

DEDUCTIONS AND CREDITS FOR S CORPORATION — 54

CHAPTER 6 — 64

COMPLIANCE AND REPORTING OBLIGATIONS — 64

CHAPTER 7   76
ADVANCED TAX PLANNING TECHNIQUES
76

CHAPTER 8   86
CASE STUDIES AND SUCCESS STORIES
86

CHAPTER 9   92
FUTURE TRENDS AND CHANGES IN S CORPORATION TAXATION   92

CHAPTER 10   100
PUTTING IT ALL TOGETHER - A COMPREHENSIVE TAX SAVINGS PLAN   100

CONCLUSION   110

Unleash the Power of S Corporation Tax Secrets

Welcome, fellow entrepreneur, to the realm of S corporation taxation—a landscape brimming with opportunity, complexity, and, if navigated wisely, immense financial rewards. As you embark on this journey with me, you're about to discover the keys to unlocking the full potential of S corporations for slashing your tax bills and propelling your business towards unprecedented growth and prosperity.

In the ever-evolving landscape of small business ownership, one thing remains constant: the quest to minimize tax liabilities while maximizing profits. It's a balancing act that requires not only a keen understanding of tax laws but also strategic planning and foresight. And that's where S corporations enter the scene as a game-changer for savvy entrepreneurs like yourself.

But what exactly is an S corporation, and why is it hailed as a powerhouse for tax savings? At its core, an S corporation is a unique entity structure that offers the combined benefits of limited liability protection and pass-through taxation. In simpler terms, it allows business owners to enjoy the liability protection of a corporation while avoiding the double taxation typically associated with traditional C corporations.

Sounds like a dream come true, right? Well, almost. While the advantages of S corporation status are indeed compelling, navigating the intricate maze of tax laws governing these entities requires a strategic approach and a deep understanding of the nuances involved. That's where this book comes in.

In "S Corporation Tax Secrets for Beginners 2024," we'll embark on a comprehensive exploration of everything you need to know to harness the full power of S corporation taxation. From demystifying the eligibility requirements and election process to uncovering advanced tax planning techniques, each chapter is designed to equip you with the knowledge and tools necessary to take control of your tax strategy and achieve long-term financial success.

But this book isn't just about theory and technical jargon. It's a practical guide filled with actionable insights, real-world examples, and expert tips garnered from years of experience in the trenches of small business ownership. Whether you're a seasoned entrepreneur looking to refine your tax strategy or a newcomer eager to learn the ropes, there's something here for everyone.

Throughout these pages, you'll discover:

- **Eligibility Requirements and Election Process:** Understand the criteria for qualifying as an S corporation and navigate the election process with confidence.
- **Deductions and Credits:** Uncover the myriad deductions and credits available to S

corporations and learn how to leverage them to your advantage.

- **Strategic Salary and Distribution Planning:** Master the art of balancing salary and distributions to optimize tax efficiency while meeting your financial goals.
- **Advanced Tax Planning Techniques:** Explore advanced strategies for long-term tax optimization and adapt to the ever-changing landscape of tax laws and regulations.

By the time you reach the final chapter, you'll emerge armed with the knowledge and confidence to tackle your tax strategy head-on and unleash the full potential of your S corporation for maximum tax savings.

So, without further ado, let's dive into the world of S corporation taxation and embark on a journey towards financial empowerment and success. Your business's future starts now.

Welcome to "S Corporation Tax Secrets for Beginners 2024."

Warm regards,
Gregory Smith.

INTRODUCTION

S Corporations stand as a strategic powerhouse for small business owners seeking to navigate the often-perplexing taxation. An S Corporation, or S Corp, is more than just a legal entity; it's a dynamic financial tool that empowers businesses to slash their tax bills and unlock the hidden potential within their financial framework.

Unlike other business structures, an S Corporation boasts a unique taxation model known as **pass-through taxation.** This means that the corporation itself does not pay federal income taxes. Instead, profits and losses are "passed through" to shareholders, who report these on their personal tax returns. The compelling nature of this approach lies in its ability to potentially reduce overall tax liability, offering a path for businesses to retain more of their hard-earned income.

However, making use of the full potential of an S Corporation involves not only understanding its advantages but also navigating its intricacies. It's a place where strategic decision-making, meticulous planning, and a nuanced understanding of tax laws come together to create a roadmap for small businesses to optimize their financial standing.

In the following chapters, we will delve into the foundations of S Corporations, clarify the mysteries of their tax implications, and equip you with strategies that have the potential to transform the way you approach taxation. Whether you're a newcomer seeking clarity or an experienced entrepreneur eager to fine-tune your tax strategy, this journey through the secrets of S Corporations promises to be a valuable exploration of maximizing tax savings and unlocking the full financial potential of your business.

The importance of tax planning for small businesses

Tax planning is a crucial aspect of financial management for small businesses. It involves strategically managing tax liabilities to minimize their overall tax burden and maximize their profits. Effective tax planning can significantly impact a small business's financial health and long-term success. Here are some of the key reasons why tax planning is important for small businesses:

1. Minimizing Tax Liabilities:

Tax planning helps small businesses identify and implement strategies to reduce their tax obligations. This can involve taking advantage of available tax deductions, credits, and exemptions. By proactively planning for taxes throughout the year, small businesses can avoid unexpected tax bills and retain more of their hard-earned income.

2. Enhancing Cash Flow:

Tax planning can help small businesses improve their cash flow by aligning their tax payments with their income streams. By carefully managing the timing of income recognition and expense deductions, businesses can ensure they have sufficient funds to cover their tax obligations without disrupting their cash flow.

3. Promoting Growth and Expansion:

Tax planning can free up resources for small businesses to invest in growth and expansion initiatives. By reducing their tax burden, businesses can allocate more funds towards hiring new employees, expanding their product offerings, or entering new markets.

4. Avoiding Penalties and Interest Charges:

Effective tax planning helps small businesses avoid costly penalties and interest charges that can arise from late or inaccurate tax filings. By staying up-to-date with tax laws and regulations and seeking professional guidance when needed, businesses can ensure they are compliant with tax requirements.

5. Gaining a Competitive Edge:

In a competitive business landscape, tax planning can provide small businesses with a competitive advantage. By minimizing their tax liabilities, businesses can lower their operating costs and offer more competitive prices for their products or services.

6. Ensuring Long-Term Financial Stability:

Tax planning is not just about immediate savings; it's about establishing a sustainable financial strategy for the long term. By incorporating tax planning into their overall financial management, small businesses can position themselves for long-term success and stability.

CHAPTER 1

UNDERSTANDING S CORPORATION

Definition of an S Corporation

An S corporation, also known as an S subchapter, is a type of corporation that has elected to pass its corporate income, losses, deductions, and credits through to its shareholders for federal tax purposes. This means that the corporation itself does not pay taxes on its income, but the shareholders are taxed on their share of the corporation's profits and losses on their personal income tax returns.

Structure of an S Corporation

An S corporation is structured similarly to a traditional C corporation, with a board of directors, officers, and shareholders. However, there are some key differences in the structure of an S corporation, including:

- **Shareholder eligibility:** As mentioned above, S corporations have restrictions on who can be shareholders. Only individuals, estates, certain trusts, and certain tax-exempt organizations can be shareholders of an S corporation.
- **One class of stock:** S corporations can only have one class of stock. This means that all shares of stock must have the same rights and privileges.
- **Pass-through taxation:** S corporations are not taxed on their income at the corporate level. Instead, the corporation's income,

losses, deductions, and credits are passed through to the shareholders, who are taxed on their share of the corporation's profits and losses on their personal income tax returns.

Advantages and Limitations of S Corporations

Advantages:

Tax Savings:

1. S Corporations have a tax setup that can be a money-saver. The business itself doesn't pay federal income tax. Instead, profits and losses pass through to the owners (shareholders), who report them on their personal tax returns. This can mean less tax hassle and potentially more money in your pocket.

Flexibility in Profit Distribution:

2. Owners of S Corporations can decide how to split up profits among themselves. This flexibility allows for strategic financial planning and can be handy for businesses with different shareholder needs.

Limited Liability:

3. Like a shield, limited liability protects S Corporation owners from being personally responsible for business debts and liabilities. Your risk is generally limited to what you invested in the company.

Attractiveness to Investors:

4. The S Corporation structure can make your business more appealing to investors. It combines the benefits of pass-through taxation with the organizational structure of a corporation, offering the best of both worlds.

Limitations:

Eligibility Restrictions:

1. Not all businesses can hop on the S Corporation train. There are restrictions on the number and type of shareholders, and everyone on board must be a U.S. citizen or resident. This can limit the options for some businesses.

Limited Growth Potential:

2. S Corporations can't have more than 100 shareholders. If your business is aiming for rapid expansion or plans to attract a large number of investors, the S Corporation structure might feel a bit cramped.

Formalities and Paperwork:

3. Like any good thing, there's some paperwork involved. S Corporations require certain formalities, like regular meetings and record-keeping. It's a bit more administrative work compared to simpler business structures.

Stricter Ownership Rules:

4. S Corporations have specific rules about who can own shares. Non-individuals, like other corporations or LLCs, can't be shareholders. This might be a limitation if you were hoping for a diverse ownership structure.

CHAPTER 2

THE BASICS OF S CORPORATION TAXATION

Pass-Through Taxation Explained

Pass-through taxation is a type of business taxation in which the income, losses, deductions, and credits of a business "pass through" to the owners' personal income tax returns. This means that the business itself does not pay taxes on its income, but the owners are taxed on their share of the business's profits and losses on their personal income tax returns.

Pass-through taxation is typically used by sole proprietorships, partnerships, LLCs that have not elected to be taxed as C corporations, and S corporations. These types of businesses are not considered separate legal entities from their owners, so the income and losses of the business are simply treated as the income and losses of the owners.

Feature	Pass-through taxation	Corporate taxation
Tax entity	Not separate from owners	Separate from owners
Taxation	Income flows through to owners' personal taxes	Income taxed at corporate level and shareholder level

Limited liability protection	Typically, not available	Available
Self-employment taxes	Yes	No
Estate planning	Can be more complex	Simpler

Here is a table summarizing the key differences between pass-through taxation and corporate taxation:

Eligibility Requirements for S Corporation Status

To qualify for S corporation status, a corporation must meet the following requirements:

- Be a domestic corporation. This means that the corporation must be incorporated in the United States.
- Have only allowable shareholders. Allowable shareholders include individuals, estates, certain trusts, and certain tax-exempt organizations. Partnerships, corporations, and non-resident alien shareholders are not eligible shareholders of S corporations.
- Have no more than 100 shareholders.

- Have only one class of stock. This means that all shares of stock must have the same rights and privileges.
- Not be an ineligible corporation. Ineligible corporations include certain financial institutions, insurance companies, and domestic international sales corporations.

Election Process for S Corporation Status

To form an S corporation, a corporation must file Form 2553 with the Internal Revenue Service (IRS). The corporation must also adopt an S corporation election agreement.

The S corporation election agreement must be signed by all of the corporation's shareholders. The agreement must also include the following information:

> The date on which the corporation wants the S election to take effect

- The name and address of the corporation
- The Employer Identification Number (EIN) of the corporation
- The number of shares of each class of stock issued by the corporation
- The name and address of each shareholder

Once the Form 2553 and the S corporation election agreement have been filed with the IRS, the corporation will be an S corporation. The S corporation election will take effect on the date that is specified on the Form 2553.

Terminating S Corporation Status

An S corporation can terminate its S election in a number of ways, including:

- Voluntarily revoking the S election: The corporation can file Form 2553 with the IRS to voluntarily revoke its S election. The revocation will take effect on the date that is specified on the Form 2553.

- Failing to meet the eligibility requirements: If an S corporation fails to meet any of the eligibility requirements, its S election will automatically terminate. The termination will take effect on the date that the corporation fails to meet the eligibility requirements.
- Having more than 100 shareholders: If an S corporation has more than 100 shareholders at the end of its taxable year, its S election will automatically terminate. The termination will take effect on the first day of the corporation's next taxable year.

CHAPTER 3

TAX BENEFITS OF S CORPORATION

Comparisons with Other Business Structures

S corporations offer a unique tax advantage over other business structures, known as pass-through taxation. This can result in significant tax savings for businesses that would otherwise be taxed at the corporate level.

To fully appreciate the tax benefits of S corporations, it is important to compare them to other common business structures, such as sole proprietorships, partnerships, LLCs, and C corporations.

Sole Proprietorships

Sole proprietorships are the simplest type of business structure, as there is no distinction between the business and the owner. This means that the owner is personally liable for all of the business's debts and liabilities, and the business's income and losses are reported on the owner's personal income tax return.

Partnerships

Partnerships are similar to sole proprietorships in that there is no separate legal entity, and the partners are personally liable for the partnership's debts and liabilities. However, partnerships are able to file their own tax returns, and the partners' share of the partnership's income and losses is reported on their personal income tax returns.

LLCs

Limited liability companies (LLCs) offer limited liability protection to their owners, but they can choose to be taxed as either sole proprietorships, partnerships, or C corporations.

C Corporations

C corporations are the most complex type of business structure, and they are taxed at the corporate level. This means that the corporation itself pays taxes on its income, and the shareholders are also taxed on their share of the corporation's dividends.

S corporations offer several tax advantages over other business structures. They avoid double taxation, which is the taxation of corporate income both at the corporate level and at the shareholder level. Additionally, S corporations offer limited liability protection to their shareholders, which means that the shareholders are not personally liable for the corporation's debts and liabilities.

However, it is important to note that S corporations are subject to additional administrative requirements, such as the filing of an S corporation election agreement and the maintenance of separate corporate records. Additionally, S corporations can only have one class of stock, and they can only have up to 100 shareholders.

let's delve into some real-world case studies to illustrate how businesses have leveraged the tax benefits of S Corporations:

1. **Case Study:** Tech Innovators, Inc.
    - *Background:* A small technology startup with three founders.

- *Choice:* Initially structured as a Sole Proprietorship, they transitioned to an S Corporation.
- *Outcome:* By becoming an S Corporation, they optimized their tax situation. The founders were able to strategically allocate income, reducing their overall tax liability. This flexibility allowed them to reinvest more funds into research and development.

2. **Case Study**: Family-Owned Retail Shop
    - *Background:* A family-operated retail business spanning two generations.
    - *Choice:* Transitioned from a C Corporation to an S Corporation.
    - *Outcome:* The shift to an S Corporation provided significant tax advantages. With pass-through taxation, the family avoided the double taxation associated with a C

Corporation. This allowed them to allocate more resources to expansion and provide additional perks to employees.

3. **Case Study:** Creative Agency Collective
    - *Background:* A collective of freelance creatives operating as a Partnership.
    - *Choice:* Restructured as an S Corporation.
    - *Outcome:* The switch to an S Corporation streamlined their tax situation. Instead of dealing with individual tax complexities, they benefited from a unified pass-through structure. This simplified their financial management and allowed for more efficient allocation of project earnings among the creative partners.

These case studies highlight the real-world impact of choosing an S Corporation structure. The flexibility in income allocation, avoidance of double taxation, and streamlined tax management contribute to the financial success and sustainability of these diverse businesses.

CHAPTER 4

STRATEGIES FOR OPTIMAL SALARIES AND DISTRIBUTION

Balancing Act for Tax Efficiency

Navigating the complexities of S corporation taxation requires careful consideration of salary and distribution strategies. Striking the right balance between these two components is crucial for optimizing tax efficiency and ensuring financial stability for the business and its shareholders.

The Significance of Salary and Distributions

A key aspect of S corporation tax planning lies in understanding the distinction between salary and distributions. Salaries are considered compensation for services rendered by shareholders-employees, while distributions represent a share of the corporation's profits that are passed through to shareholders.

Salary Considerations

The salary paid to shareholder-employees plays a significant role in determining the corporation's taxable income and the shareholders' tax obligations. By strategically adjusting salaries, businesses can minimize their overall tax burden.

Factors Influencing Salary Determination

Several factors should be considered when determining appropriate salaries for shareholder-employees, including:

- **Market Rates**: Salaries should be comparable to those paid to individuals with

similar qualifications and experience in the same industry and geographic region.
- **Services Rendered**: The value of services provided by the shareholder-employee should be accurately reflected in their salary.
- **Tax Considerations**: Salaries should be structured to minimize the corporation's taxable income and the shareholders' overall tax burden.

Distribution Strategies

Distributions represent the portion of the corporation's profits that are passed through to shareholders. While distributions are not subject to corporate income tax, they are taxed at the shareholders' individual income tax rates.

Timing of Distributions

The timing of distributions can significantly impact cash flow and tax implications. Businesses should carefully consider their financial needs and tax planning goals when determining the timing of distributions.

Special Distribution Considerations

Certain factors may warrant special consideration when determining distributions, such as:

- Retained Earnings: Businesses should maintain a sufficient level of retained earnings to cover operational expenses and potential contingencies.
- Shareholder Equity: Distributions should be allocated fairly among shareholders in accordance with their ownership interests.
- Tax Implications: Distributions should be structured to minimize the shareholders' overall tax burden.

Optimal Salary and Distribution Balance

The optimal balance between salary and distributions depends on the specific circumstances of each business and its shareholders. However, the general rule of thumb suggests allocating 60% of profits to salary and 40% to distributions. This approach aims to minimize the corporation's taxable income while providing shareholders with a reasonable return on their investment.

Impact on Shareholders' Income

As we explore strategies for managing salaries and distributions within an S Corporation, it's essential to understand how these decisions impact the income of shareholders—the individuals at the heart of the corporation.

1. Reasonable Salary and Shareholder Income:

- Setting a reasonable salary strikes a balance between fair compensation and tax efficiency. Shareholders receive income through salaries, managing payroll taxes while ensuring adequate compensation.

2. Tax-Efficient Distributions and Shareholder Income:

- Planning distributions strategically influences the income shareholders receive. By optimizing distributions, shareholders can minimize tax liabilities, allowing more income to flow to them outside the realm of employment taxes.

3. Regular Review and Adjustment:

- Regularly reviewing and adjusting salaries and distributions aligns with the evolving financial health of the business and its shareholders. Shareholders benefit from a compensation strategy that adapts to changes, optimizing their income in line with the business's performance.

4. **Fringe Benefits and Shareholder Income**:

- Providing tax-efficient fringe benefits contributes to the overall compensation package. Shareholders receive additional perks, such as health insurance, enhancing their overall income without incurring heavy tax burdens.

5. **Utilization of Retained Earnings**:

- Strategically using retained earnings can impact the availability of funds for shareholders. Shareholders may benefit from reinvested earnings, supporting business growth and potentially leading to increased future distributions.

CHAPTER 5

DEDUCTIONS AND CREDITS FOR S CORPORATION

Deductions in S Corporations

Deductions are expenses that S corporations can subtract from their taxable income to reduce their tax liability. Deductions can be broadly categorized into two main types:

1. <u>Business deductions</u>: These deductions are incurred in the ordinary course of running a business and are directly related to the business's income-generating activities. Examples of business deductions include rent, utilities, salaries, supplies, travel, depreciation, and amortization.

2. <u>Employee-related deductions:</u> These deductions are related to the compensation and benefits provided to employees. Examples of employee-related deductions include health insurance premiums, retirement plan contributions, and social security and Medicare taxes.

If an S Corporation earns $100,000 in revenue but has $20,000 in deductible expenses, the taxable income is calculated as $100,000 - $20,000 = $80,000.

Eligibility for Deductions

To be eligible for a deduction, the expense must be:

- Ordinary and necessary: The expense must be reasonable and customary for businesses in the same industry.
- Paid or incurred during the taxable year: The expense must have been paid or incurred during the taxable year for which the deduction is being claimed.
- Incurred in carrying on the trade or business: The expense must be directly related to the business's income-generating activities.

Claiming Deductions

S corporations claim deductions on their Form 1120-S, U.S. Corporation Income Tax Return. The form provides specific lines for claiming various types of deductions. S corporations should maintain accurate records of all expenses to support their deduction claims.

Impact of Deductions

Deductions can significantly reduce an S corporation's taxable income, thereby lowering its tax liability. This can result in increased cash flow and improved profitability for the business.

Maximizing Deductions and Credits

S corporations, like other business entities, are eligible for a variety of deductions and credits that can help reduce their tax liability. By understanding and utilizing these available tax benefits, S corporations can effectively manage their tax obligations and enhance their financial performance.

Key Deductions for S Corporations

Several deductions are particularly beneficial for S corporations, including:

- Business expenses: S corporations can deduct the ordinary and necessary expenses incurred in carrying on their trade or business. This includes expenses such as rent, utilities, salaries, supplies, and travel.
- Depreciation and amortization: S corporations can deduct the depreciation and amortization of tangible property used in their business. This allows businesses to recover the cost of these assets over time.
- Interest expense: S corporations can deduct interest paid on loans used to finance their business operations. This includes interest on loans used to purchase equipment, inventory, or real estate.
- Health insurance premiums: S corporations can deduct premiums paid for health insurance coverage for their employees. This

includes premiums for medical, dental, and vision insurance.

- Retirement plan contributions: S corporations can deduct contributions made to retirement plans for their employees, such as 401(k) plans and profit-sharing plans.

Maximizing Deductions and Credits

To maximize deductions and credits, S corporations should:

- Keep accurate and detailed records of all expenses: This will make it easier to identify and claim eligible deductions on their tax returns.
- Stay up-to-date on tax law changes: Tax laws can change frequently, so it is important to stay informed of any changes that may affect deductions and credits for S corporations.
- Seek professional guidance: Tax professionals can provide valuable advice on maximizing deductions and credits and ensuring compliance with tax laws.

Common Credits for S Corporations

In addition to deductions, S corporations may also be eligible for certain tax credits, such as:

- Foreign tax credit: S corporations that pay taxes to foreign countries may be eligible for a credit against their U.S. tax liability.
- Employment tax credit: S corporations that hire new employees may be eligible for a credit against their federal employment taxes.
- Work opportunity tax credit: S corporations that hire individuals from certain disadvantaged groups may be eligible for a credit against their federal income tax liability.
- Research and development credit: S corporations that incur expenses related to research and development activities may be

eligible for a credit against their federal income tax liability.

CHAPTER 6

COMPLIANCE AND REPORTING OBLIGATIONS

<u>Meeting IRS Requirements</u>

S corporations, like all businesses, are subject to various compliance and reporting obligations imposed by the Internal Revenue Service (IRS). These obligations ensure that S corporations accurately report their income, pay taxes, and maintain proper records. Failure to comply with these obligations can result in penalties and other adverse consequences.

Key Compliance and Reporting Obligations for S Corporations

1. **Filing Form 1120-S:** S corporations must file Form 1120-S, U.S. Corporation Income Tax Return, annually. This form reports the corporation's income, deductions, credits, and distributions to shareholders.

2. **Maintaining Separate Corporate Records**: S corporations must maintain separate corporate records from the personal records of their shareholders. This includes records of income, expenses, assets, liabilities, and shareholder transactions.

3. **Paying Estimated Taxes**: S corporations are required to make estimated tax payments throughout the year to avoid penalties. These payments are based on the corporation's estimated tax liability.

4. **Filing Form 2553:** S corporations must file Form 2553, Election by a Small Business

Corporation, to make an S corporation election. This election must be filed with the IRS within two months and fifteen days of the beginning of the taxable year for which the election is to be effective.

5. **Providing Shareholders with Schedule K-1:** S corporations must provide Schedule K-1, Shareholder's Share of Income, Deductions, Credits, etc., to their shareholders annually. This schedule reports each shareholder's share of the corporation's income, deductions, credits, and distributions.

Additional Compliance Considerations

In addition to these core obligations, S corporations may have additional compliance requirements depending on their specific activities and circumstances. These may include:

- State and Local Taxes: S corporations may be subject to state and local taxes, such as state income taxes, franchise taxes, and sales taxes.
- Employment Taxes: S corporations must withhold and pay federal employment taxes, such as Social Security and Medicare taxes, on behalf of their employees.
- Pension and Retirement Plan Requirements: If S corporations offer pension or retirement plans to their employees, they may be subject to specific regulatory requirements.
- Industry-Specific Regulations: S corporations operating in certain industries

may be subject to additional compliance requirements specific to their industry.

Importance of Compliance

Compliance with IRS requirements is crucial for S corporations for several reasons:

- Avoiding Penalties and Interest: Failure to comply with tax laws and reporting obligations can result in significant penalties and interest charges.
- Maintaining Tax Status: S corporations must maintain compliance to retain their S corporation status and avoid double taxation of corporate income.
- Protecting Shareholders: Proper recordkeeping and tax filings help protect shareholders from personal liability for the corporation's debts and taxes.

- Ensuring Financial Stability: Compliance fosters transparency and accountability, contributing to the corporation's overall financial stability.

Avoiding common pitfalls

Avoiding common pitfalls is essential for any business, and S corporations are no exception. By understanding and proactively addressing potential issues, S corporations can safeguard their financial health and protect themselves from legal and tax complications.

Common Pitfalls for S Corporations

1. Failure to Elect S Corporation Status Properly: S corporation status must be elected correctly and timely to avoid double taxation and other adverse consequences. It is crucial to consult with a tax professional to ensure proper election and compliance with eligibility requirements.
2. Inadequate Recordkeeping: Proper recordkeeping is essential for S corporations to track income, expenses, assets, liabilities,

and shareholder transactions. Failure to maintain accurate records can lead to tax disputes, financial mismanagement, and difficulty in resolving legal issues.

3. Mischaracterization of Compensation: S corporations must carefully distinguish between salary and distributions to avoid tax penalties and maintain compliance with employment tax laws. Improperly classifying compensation can result in underpayment of taxes and potential liability for the corporation and its shareholders.

4. Disregard of Corporate Formalities: S corporations must maintain a clear separation between the corporation and its shareholders to protect shareholders from personal liability. Blending personal and corporate transactions can lead to the "piercing of the corporate veil," exposing shareholders to the corporation's debts and liabilities.

5. Failure to Follow Distribution Rules: S corporations must follow specific rules regarding the distribution of profits to shareholders. Improper distributions can trigger tax liabilities and disrupt financial planning.
6. Neglecting Tax Obligations: S corporations are subject to various tax obligations, including estimated tax payments, payroll tax withholding, and annual tax filings. Failure to meet these obligations can result in penalties, interest charges, and potential revocation of S corporation status.
7. Unclear Shareholder Agreements: S corporations should have clearly defined shareholder agreements that outline ownership rights, responsibilities, and dispute resolution procedures. Lack of clear agreements can lead to conflicts, misunderstandings, and legal disputes.

8. Inadequate Insurance Coverage: S corporations should obtain adequate insurance coverage to protect against potential liabilities, such as property damage, employee injuries, and professional malpractice. Insufficient insurance can leave the corporation and its shareholders exposed to financial losses.

Strategies for Avoiding Pitfalls

1. Seek Professional Guidance: Consult with qualified tax professionals and business advisors to ensure compliance with tax laws, corporate formalities, and best practices for managing an S corporation.
2. Establish Clear Policies and Procedures: Develop clear policies and procedures for various aspects of the business, including compensation, distributions, recordkeeping, and shareholder communication.
3. Maintain Regular Communication: Foster open and transparent communication among shareholders and management to address issues promptly and prevent misunderstandings.
4. Conduct Regular Reviews: Regularly review financial statements, tax records, and corporate governance practices to identify

potential issues and take corrective action as needed.

5. Seek Expert Advice When Needed: Consult with legal counsel for complex matters involving shareholder agreements, employment contracts, or potential litigation.

CHAPTER 7

Advanced tax planning techniques

<u>Leveraging S Corporation Nuances</u>

In this chapter, we'll delve into advanced tax planning techniques—specifically, how to leverage the unique nuances of S Corporations for strategic financial advantage.

1. S Corporation Salary vs. Distributions Optimization:

- What it Means: Fine-tune the balance between salaries and distributions to optimize tax benefits.
- Why it Matters: Strategic planning of how owners are compensated can significantly impact overall tax liabilities.

2. Timing of Income Recognition:

- What it Means: Carefully manage when the S Corporation recognizes income.
- Why it Matters: Timing can influence the tax rate at which income is taxed, offering opportunities for tax savings.

3. Debt Basis Planning:

- What it Means: Utilize debt basis planning to enhance the deductibility of losses.
- Why it Matters: Strategic use of debt can increase the amount of losses shareholders can deduct on their individual tax returns.

4. Cost Segregation Studies:

- What it Means: Undertake cost segregation studies to identify accelerated depreciation opportunities.
- Why it Matters: Accelerated depreciation can result in larger deductions in the earlier years, providing immediate tax benefits.

5. Charitable Remainder Trusts (CRTs):

- What it Means: Explore the use of CRTs to facilitate tax-advantaged charitable giving.
- Why it Matters: CRTs allow for charitable contributions while potentially providing income streams and tax advantages for the donor.

6. Estate Freeze Strategies:

- What it Means: Implement estate freeze strategies to lock in the current value of the business for estate tax purposes.
- Why it Matters: Protecting the business's value can lead to reduced estate taxes for future generations.

7. Utilizing Section 1244 Stock:

- What it Means: Consider the issuance of Section 1244 stock for potential ordinary loss treatment.
- Why it Matters: This can be advantageous in the event of a business loss, providing a potential tax benefit.

8. Qualified Small Business Stock (QSBS):

- What it Means: Explore the benefits of holding QSBS for potential capital gains exclusions.
- Why it Matters: Holding qualifying stock can lead to significant tax advantages upon sale.

Long-term tax optimization strategies are designed to minimize tax liabilities over an extended period, ensuring financial stability and maximizing wealth accumulation. These strategies involve a comprehensive approach that considers various factors, including income, expenses, investments, and retirement planning.

Key Long-Term Tax Optimization Strategies

1. Choose the Right Business Structure: Selecting the most suitable business

structure, such as sole proprietorship, partnership, LLC, or corporation, can significantly impact tax obligations. Each structure has distinct tax implications, so careful evaluation is crucial.

2. Maximize Tax-Deductible Expenses: Identify and claim all eligible deductions to reduce taxable income. This includes expenses such as business travel, meals, supplies, and depreciation of assets.

3. Leverage Retirement Savings Plans: Contribute to retirement plans, such as 401(k)s and IRAs, to defer taxes on contributions and earnings until retirement. These plans offer significant tax benefits and contribute to long-term financial security.

4. Consider Tax-Efficient Investments: Prioritize tax-advantaged investments, such as municipal bonds and qualified dividend-paying stocks, to minimize tax burdens on investment income.

5. Engage in Tax-Loss Harvesting: Strategically sell losing investments to offset capital gains and reduce overall tax liabilities. This technique can be particularly beneficial during periods of market volatility.
6. Plan for Estate Taxes: Implement estate planning strategies, such as creating trusts and gifting assets, to minimize estate taxes and ensure a smooth transfer of wealth to heirs.

Additional Considerations for Long-Term Tax Optimization

1. Regular Tax Review: Conduct periodic reviews of tax strategies to adapt to changes in tax laws and personal circumstances.
2. Seek Professional Guidance: Consult with qualified tax professionals, such as certified public accountants (CPAs) or tax attorneys,

to develop and implement tailored tax optimization plans.

3. Maintain Accurate Records: Keep meticulous records of income, expenses, investments, and tax-related documents to support tax filings and ensure compliance.

CHAPTER 8

Case Studies and Success Stories

Here are some real-world examples of businesses that have thrived using S corporation strategies:

1. Medical Practice: A medical practice with five physician-owners converted from a partnership to an S corporation. By doing so, the practice was able to avoid double taxation and save over $100,000 in taxes per year. The practice was also able to offer limited liability protection to its owners, which was a major concern for the physicians.

2. Retail Store: A retail store with 20 employees converted from a sole proprietorship to an S corporation. By doing so, the owner was able to avoid double taxation and save over $50,000 in

taxes per year. The owner was also able to offer limited liability protection to themselves, which was a major concern for the owner.

3. Software Company: A software company with 100 employees converted from a C corporation to an S corporation. By doing so, the company was able to avoid double taxation and save over $1 million in taxes per year. The company was also able to offer limited liability protection to its shareholders, which was a major concern for the company's investors.

4. Real Estate Investment Company: A real estate investment company with multiple properties converted from a C corporation to an S corporation. By doing so, the company was able to avoid double taxation and save over $1 million in taxes per year. The company was also able to pass through depreciation deductions to its

shareholders, which significantly reduced their tax liabilities.

5. Professional Services Firm: A professional services firm with 50 partners converted from a partnership to an S corporation. By doing so, the partnership was able to avoid double taxation and save over $200,000 in taxes per year. The partners were also able to offer limited liability protection to themselves, which was a major concern for the partners.

These examples highlight the potential tax savings and other benefits that businesses can achieve by converting to an S corporation and implementing effective S corporation strategies. However, it is important to note that S corporations are not suitable for all businesses. Businesses should carefully consider their specific circumstances and consult with a tax advisor to determine if an S corporation is the right choice for them.

Here are some key lessons that can be learned from these real-world examples:

- Proper Planning and Execution: Successful S corporation strategies require careful planning and execution. Businesses should consider their specific circumstances and goals before converting to an S corporation.
- Professional Guidance: Consulting with a qualified tax advisor is essential for understanding the tax implications of converting to an S corporation and developing effective tax strategies.
- Regular Review and Adjustments: S corporation strategies should be reviewed regularly to ensure they remain aligned with the company's financial goals and any changes in tax laws.
- Communication and Transparency: Open communication and transparency among shareholders and management are crucial for

maintaining effective S corporation governance and avoiding potential conflicts.
- Continuous Learning and Adaptation: The tax landscape is constantly evolving, so it is important for businesses to stay informed about changes in tax laws and adapt their strategies accordingly.

By following these lessons and implementing sound S corporation strategies, businesses can maximize the benefits of this unique business structure and achieve long-term financial success.

CHAPTER 9

Future Trends and Changes in S Corporation Taxation

Potential Legislative Developments

The S corporation tax landscape is constantly evolving due to changes in tax laws and economic conditions. It is important for businesses to stay informed about potential legislative developments that could impact their S corporation status and tax obligations.

Potential Legislative Changes

Here are some potential legislative changes that could impact S corporation taxation:

- Changes to the S corporation eligibility requirements: The IRS could modify the eligibility requirements for S corporations, such as increasing the maximum number of shareholders or restricting certain types of businesses from electing S status.
- Modifications to the pass-through deduction: The pass-through deduction, which allows S corporations to pass through certain deductions to their shareholders, could be modified or eliminated. This could significantly impact the tax benefits of S corporations.
- Changes to the taxation of dividends: Dividends paid by S corporations are currently taxed at the shareholder's ordinary income tax rate. The IRS could change this to a more favorable tax rate or eliminate the tax altogether.
- Increased scrutiny of S corporations: The IRS could increase its scrutiny of S

corporations to ensure compliance with tax laws and prevent abuse of the S corporation structure. This could lead to more audits and enforcement actions.

Impact of Potential Changes

Potential legislative changes could have a significant impact on S corporations. Businesses should carefully consider the potential impact of these changes on their tax liabilities and financial planning.

Adapting to Change

To adapt to potential legislative changes, businesses should:

- Stay informed about tax law changes: Regularly review tax updates and consult with tax professionals to stay informed about changes in S corporation taxation.
- Evaluate the impact of changes: Analyze the potential impact of legislative changes on their specific business and financial situation.
- Adjust tax strategies as needed: Make necessary adjustments to their tax strategies to maintain compliance and minimize tax liabilities.
- Seek professional guidance: Consult with qualified tax advisors to develop and implement strategies to adapt to changing tax laws.

Adapting to an evolving tax landscape is crucial for businesses to maintain compliance, minimize tax liabilities, and achieve long-term financial success. Here are some key strategies for businesses to adapt to changes in tax laws:

1. Stay Informed: Continuously monitor tax updates and changes in legislation by subscribing to tax publications, attending tax seminars, and consulting with qualified tax professionals.
2. Evaluate the Impact: Analyze the potential impact of tax law changes on the business's financial situation, tax liabilities, and overall operations.
3. Proactive Planning: Anticipate potential tax law changes and proactively plan for their impact by evaluating different scenarios and developing contingency strategies.
4. Review and Update Tax Strategies: Regularly review existing tax strategies to

ensure they align with current tax laws and adapt them as needed to minimize tax liabilities.
5. Seek Professional Guidance: Consult with qualified tax advisors to gain insights into complex tax regulations, develop effective tax mitigation strategies, and ensure compliance with tax laws.
6. Maintain Accurate Records: Keep meticulous records of income, expenses, deductions, credits, and other relevant tax information to support tax filings and facilitate audits.
7. Communicate Effectively: Communicate tax law changes and their implications to employees, shareholders, and other stakeholders to ensure transparency and informed decision-making.
8. Embrace Technology: Utilize tax software and online resources to streamline tax

preparation, automate tasks, and stay updated on tax law changes.

9. Monitor Industry Trends: Stay informed about industry-specific tax trends and regulations to adapt tax strategies accordingly and maintain a competitive edge.

10. Continuous Learning: Commit to continuous learning by attending tax conferences, webinars, and workshops to enhance tax knowledge and stay up-to-date on the latest tax developments.

CHAPTER 10

Putting it all together - A comprehensive tax savings plan

Creating a customized tax plan for your business is essential to minimize tax liabilities, optimize financial performance, and ensure long-term success. A well-structured tax plan should be tailored to the specific circumstances of your business, considering factors such as industry, business structure, income sources, expenses, and tax goals.

Key Steps to Creating a Customized Tax Plan

1. Evaluate Your Business: Conduct a thorough assessment of your business, including its industry, legal structure,

income streams, expenses, tax history, and financial goals.

2. Identify Taxable Income Sources: Accurately identify all sources of taxable income for your business, including revenue from sales, investments, and other activities.

3. Determine Deductible Expenses: Identify and categorize all deductible expenses incurred in the operation of your business, such as rent, utilities, salaries, supplies, and depreciation.

4. Analyze Tax Credits and Deductions: Research and identify all applicable tax credits and deductions that your business may be eligible for, such as the Small Business Health Care Tax Credit or the Employment Tax Credit.

5. Choose the Right Tax Structure: Consider your business goals and tax implications when selecting the appropriate tax structure,

such as sole proprietorship, partnership, LLC, or corporation.

6. Establish Tax Goals: Set clear and realistic tax goals that align with your business's overall financial objectives, such as minimizing tax liabilities or maximizing tax credits.

7. Project Tax Liabilities: Estimate your business's potential tax liabilities based on current tax laws, your projected income, and eligible deductions and credits.

8. Develop Tax Strategies: Formulate strategic approaches to minimize tax liabilities, such as deferring income, maximizing deductions, and utilizing tax-advantaged investments.

9. Seek Professional Guidance: Consult with qualified tax professionals, such as certified public accountants (CPAs) or tax attorneys, to develop a comprehensive tax plan tailored to your business's unique needs.

Benefits of a Customized Tax Plan

A customized tax plan can provide numerous benefits for your business, including:

1. Reduced Tax Liabilities: By effectively utilizing tax strategies and maximizing deductions and credits, you can minimize your business's tax burden and increase your net income.
2. Improved Financial Performance: A well-structured tax plan can optimize your business's financial performance by reducing tax expenses and enhancing cash flow.
3. Enhanced Compliance: A customized tax plan ensures compliance with current tax laws, reducing the risk of audits and penalties.
4. Proactive Planning: A well-defined tax plan allows for proactive planning and informed

decision-making, enabling you to anticipate tax implications and adapt to changes in tax laws.

5. Business Growth and Sustainability: A customized tax plan contributes to long-term business growth and sustainability by ensuring financial stability and minimizing tax roadblocks.

here is an example of a customized tax plan for a small business:

Business: ABC Consulting, LLC

Industry: Consulting services

Tax Structure: S corporation

Tax Goals:

1. Minimize tax liabilities
2. Maximize tax credits and deductions
3. Ensure compliance with current tax laws

Tax Strategies:

1. Defer income by delaying invoicing until the following tax year
2. Maximize deductions by tracking all business expenses and maintaining detailed records
3. Utilize tax-advantaged investments, such as retirement plans, to defer taxes on income
4. Take advantage of tax credits, such as the Small Business Health Care Tax Credit and the Employment Tax Credit

Projected Tax Liabilities:

Based on current tax laws, ABC Consulting's estimated tax liability for the current year is $50,000. By implementing the tax strategies outlined above, the company expects to reduce its tax liability to $30,000.

Action Plan:

1. Implement a system for tracking all business income and expenses
2. Establish a monthly or quarterly review process to monitor tax liabilities and adjust strategies as needed
3. Consult with a tax professional on an annual basis to review the tax plan and ensure compliance with current tax laws

Expected Outcomes:

By implementing this customized tax plan, ABC Consulting expects to achieve the following outcomes:

1. Reduce its annual tax liability by $20,000
2. Increase its net income by $15,000
3. Enhance its financial performance and cash flow
4. Ensure compliance with current tax laws

Conclusion

This example demonstrates how a customized tax plan can be tailored to the specific needs of a small business to achieve its financial goals and ensure long-term success. By carefully considering the business's industry, tax structure, income sources, expenses, and tax goals, a well-structured tax plan can significantly reduce tax liabilities, optimize financial performance, and contribute to the overall growth and sustainability of the business.

Conclusion

As you conclude this book on S corporations, I want to encourage you, as a small business owner, to embrace the power of effective tax planning and strategic financial management. While navigating the complexities of tax laws and financial regulations can be daunting, the rewards of optimizing your business's tax position and achieving long-term financial stability are well worth the effort.

Remember, you are not alone in this journey. There are numerous resources available to help you, including qualified tax professionals, business advisors, and government agencies that provide guidance and support to small businesses.

Here are some key takeaways to keep in mind as you move forward:

1. Stay informed about tax laws: Keep abreast of changes in tax laws and regulations to ensure your business remains compliant and takes advantage of available tax benefits.
2. Seek professional guidance: Consult with qualified tax professionals to develop a customized tax plan tailored to your business's unique needs and goals.
3. Maintain accurate records: Keep meticulous records of income, expenses, deductions, credits, and other relevant tax information to support tax filings and facilitate audits.
4. Plan for the future: Anticipate future tax implications and make informed decisions that align with your long-term financial objectives.
5. Embrace continuous learning: Continuously seek opportunities to enhance your tax

knowledge and stay updated on the latest tax developments.

By following these principles and actively managing your business's tax affairs, you can effectively minimize tax liabilities, optimize financial performance, and pave the way for long-term success and growth.

duct-compliance